A guide to the most romantic clubs, restaurants, bars, and hotels in San Francisco

ROMANTIC SAN FRANCISCO

PHOTOGRAPHS BY JIMMY HAHN

TEXT BY WILLIAM KING III

Thousands of people, thousands of places to eat and drink, yet too often a quandary: *Where can we go for a private interlude, a space to call our own, a place to be together? Some place, well, romantic.*

Romantic San Francisco reveals the places and the spaces the savviest San Franciscans know about, but like to keep to themselves.

CONTENTS

Romantic Hotels

Romantic Dinners

Romantic Brunches

Romantic Rendezvous

Credits

The Archbishop's Mansion

1000 FULTON STREET (415) 563-7872

The Archbishop's Mansion calls to mind the 1978 Goldie Hawn/Chevy Chase comedy caper, *Foul Play,* in which Chevy and Goldie unwillingly becoming entangled in a complex plan by an evil archdiocese to assassinate the Pope during his visit to San Francisco. The malevolent scheme is operated out of what is supposed to be an archbishop's mansion. The real Archbishop's Mansion was built in 1904 as a residence for Archbishop Patrick Riordan. Subsequently "de-commissioned" by the church, the house has served since 1983 as a fifteen-room bed-and-breakfast. The mansion was crafted in the Belle Époque style and is furnished with an eclectic mix of fine European antiques. No room resembles another, but all have been christened with the names of well-known operas, such as *Don Giovanni* and *Carmen.* Distinctive in style and feel, The Archbishop's Mansion is more likely to generate visions of the high-ranking churchmen who trod its historic hallways than of Goldie and Chevy's madcap chases.

Hotel Bohème

444 COLUMBUS AVENUE (415) 433-9111

Had Pablo Picasso, Jean Cocteau, and the Beatniks pooled their ideas and come together to open a small fifteen-room hotel, they very well could have conceived the Hotel Bohème. At the very least, all would feel comfortable spending time in San Francisco interior designer Candra Scott's bohemian hideaway in North Beach. In European style, the Hotel Bohème keeps its operation small and personalized. Visitors can peruse the romantic black and white photographs depicting nocturnal images of San Francisco in the hallways. Guest rooms are furnished with wicker chairs, bistro tables, and black iron beds covered in Vichy checkered duvets. The Hotel Bohème's warm colors and artsy detail recreate a jazzy vibe that was made famous in this area almost forty years ago.

Hotel Bijou

111 MASON STREET (415) 771-1200

When you check into the Hotel Bijou, it may feel as if you will be spending the night in a movie theater. To some extent, you will be. The concierge desk looks more like a concession stand than, well, a concierge desk. Sure, you can get your room keys there and pay your bill, but you can also buy goodies to snack on if you choose to view one of the two nightly features in the Bijou's private screening room. Each film featured at the Bijou was shot in the San Francisco area. The hotel is decorated with Hollywood memorabilia, and each room is christened with the title of a film shot in — you guessed it — San Francisco. This cinematic theme is carried through with a touch of class — the Bijou is no Planet Hollywood facsimile. And unlike the price of movie tickets these days, the Hotel Bijou is matinee affordable.

Hotel Monaco

501 GEARY STREET (AT TAYLOR) (415) 292-0100

It's fun to imagine what traveling must have been like for the wealthy during the early part of the twentieth century. They could relax in luxurious accommodations after touring the globe in high style. San Francisco's Hotel Monaco does an impressive job of reviving this era for today's traveler. As if it were a backdrop for an F. Scott Fitzgerald novel, the Monaco has spared no effort in re-creating the elegance and style of a time now gone. With decorative influences from many cultures and every continent, San Francisco's Hotel Monaco rivals the Ritz Hotel of Paris and the St. Regis in New York — at a fraction of the cost. A large 1920's steamer trunk appropriately functions as a registration desk. The impressive grand lobby awes guests with its marble staircase, lavish furniture, and two-story fireplace. Travelers from every nation will feel at home in rooms where the warm colors, cozy fabrics, and choice furnishings speak a universal language.

Hotel Rex

562 SUTTER STREET (415) 433-4434

The famed Algonquin Hotel in New York was the first famous hangout for the literary lights of the early twentieth century. In recent years San Francisco has had the West Coast equivalent, the Hotel Rex. The intelligentsia will surely feel at home in the Rex's clubby, library-like lobby surrounded by Cubist paintings, vintage black dial phones, leather-bound books, and a classic zinc bar. The hotel's lobby and guest rooms are filled with sophisticated art and furnishings produced or inspired by writers and painters, many of whom are in some way affiliated with San Francisco's notable artistic and intellectual history. The rooms and particularly the hotel's suites have the feel of tastefully decorated apartments and boast carefully chosen art collections. A few days at the Hotel Rex could inspire you to write the Great American Novel or take up painting.

Hotel Triton

342 GRANT AVENUE (AT BUSH STREET) (415) 394-0500

New York has The Royalton. Paris has The Hotel Costes. London has The Metropolitan. So how does San Francisco fare in the battle of fashionable hotels? With its originality of design and unconventional spirit, San Francisco's wonderfully funky Triton competes with any of the others. Were it not a hotel, the Triton would undisputedly be an ultra-hip advertising agency. With a conference room dubbed the "creative zone," single-bed guest rooms referred to as "Zen dens," and "celebrity suites" with personal decorative touches by the likes of Jerry Garcia and Carlos Santana, the Triton has had as much thought and creative energy devoted to it as a great Apple Computer ad campaign. Few other hotels can boast an "eco floor" furnished in tribute to Mother Nature, with naturally grown cotton bed linens, biodegradable hair and skincare products, and air-purifying systems. For those in search of romance, the Triton offers a weekend romance package complete with a can of whipped cream, edible undies, and massage oils.

The Mansions Hotel

2220 SACRAMENTO STREET (AT LAGUNA STREET) (415) 929-9444

San Francisco has long been considered a city with liberal attitudes. It is, therefore, a magnet for people with peculiar, and sometimes bizarre, tastes. This may be best demonstrated through a visit to The Mansions Hotel. The *San Francisco Examiner* once said of the place, "The Mansions is San Francisco's most San Francisco hotel." If you didn't know better, you might think that The Mansions is much like the other Victorian hotels scattered across the city. However, closer inquiry will reveal that it is more like the Bates Motel or Madame Tussaud's Wax Museum. This may be because The Mansions is famed for its Magic Show and Dinner. Or perhaps it is the collection of pig memorabilia that fills one entire room that lends a special air to The Mansions. It could also have something to do with the hotel's concierge, who strolls around with a parrot on his shoulder. There is such a weird and fascinatingly eclectic mix of antiques and collectibles displayed throughout the hotel that one visit is not sufficient to see it all. Many celebrities, from DeNiro to JFK, Jr., have passed through The Mansions and left their John Hancock on a wall dedicated to fame. Maybe they were drawn here because they heard that The Mansions is such a beautifully haunting experience.

The Phoenix Hotel

601 ADDY STREET (AT LARKIN STREET) (415) 776-1380

The Phoenix Hotel is a fashionable version of the innumerable motels scattered across America, usually situated off exit ramps in the middle of nowhere, that any weary driver will inevitably stumble upon during a cross-country trip. The Phoenix was originally conceived as a comfortable "crash pad" for touring rock and roll bands who play gigs in San Francisco. In essence, it is a playground where musicians can unwind from hectic tour schedules in the comfort of a tropically themed room, a funky outdoor pool, or the ultra-cool Backflip bar and restaurant. It is a far cry from The Four Seasons, but this hasn't kept marquee names such as REM and The Red Hot Chili Peppers from passing time at the infamous motel. You do not, however, need a backstage pass or a tour bus to participate in the fun at The Phoenix. In fact, The Phoenix might be one of the few places left in the world where fans can actually mingle freely with rock and roll icons.

The Sherman House

2160 GREEN STREET (415) 563-3600

Pretend you are a celebrity — a movie star, a politician, a corporate raider. The point is that you crave a few moments away from the spotlight, except that you need, even demand, the pampering and excellent service you have come to expect. This being your fortunate situation, it would be wise to consider a getaway weekend at the luxurious Sherman House. This beautiful, fourteen-room, white Victorian home is the ultimate hideaway for the rich and famous. Rooms of varying styles, sizes, and prices are available to choose from — that is, *if* you can get a reservation. Canopied beds, woodburning fireplaces, reading alcoves, and grand terraces with spectacular views of San Francisco Bay are just a few of the elegant amenities available to guests of The Sherman House. Its chateau-like quality, exquisite dining, manicured gardens, and top-notch staff make it unlikely that other hotels can match its magnificence.

Spencer House

1080 HAIGHT STREET (AT BAKER STREET) (415) 626-9205

Everyone who visits San Francisco notices the city's ubiquitous and beautiful Victorian homes. As recognizable as the Transamerica Building or the Golden Gate Bridge, the San Francisco Victorian home is clearly an important part of the city's romantic charm. Directly across the street from Buena Vista Park stands a remarkable Queen Anne residence known as the Spencer House. Originally constructed in 1887 for John C. Spencer, the home now serves as a charming bed and breakfast hotel. There are but six coveted rooms in the Spencer House, each with its own personality: the French Room, the Garden Room, the Victorian Room, to name only half. The house is pleasantly done up in period antiques and has been restored to its original Victorian style, thus immersing guests in a bygone era of this unique American city.

Absinthe Brasserie and Bar

398 HAYES STREET (AT GOUGH STREET) (415) 551-1590

At the last turn of the century, French poets, painters, and writers such as Rimbaud, Toulouse-Lautrec, and Baudelaire spent endless hours at Parisian bistros sipping the anise-flavored liqueur known as absinthe. The potent drink subsequently fell out of favor, but its memory is evoked at San Francisco's Absinthe Brasserie and Bar. Nothing as strong as absinthe is available at the restaurant's bar, but don't let this deter you from dropping by this Hayes Valley hot spot. Styled as a French brasserie, Absinthe interprets the concept by offering both casual and formal dining arrangements. In the front by the bar, patrons can take a seat at a traditional café table and order from a simple but good bistro menu in a relaxed atmosphere. The more formal rear space is preferable for special evenings out. The warm ambiance is completed by sleek banquettes and colorful murals depicting scenes from the Belle Époque. Wherever you dine, an evening at Absinthe will leave you feeling intoxicated.

Bistro Clovis

1596 MARKET STREET (AT FRANKLIN STREET) (415) 864-0231

With dozens of French restaurants to choose from in the San Francisco Bay area, Bistro Clovis stands out because of its refreshing lack of pretension. This unassuming Civic Center bistro is unobtrusively situated on Market Street, where curious passersby will be struck by the quaint, romantic, even serene setting that awaits them inside. In terms of decor, Bistro Clovis truly captures the essence of dining as it is experienced in France. French music plays softly over speakers in a room done up with French banquettes, lace curtains, and white linen tablecloths. Diners can enjoy the astonishingly good and imaginative dishes created by the Bistro Clovis kitchen. Bistro Clovis takes pride in its wines, exposing its patrons to a select assortment of France's own pride and joy, Le Vin.

Bix

56 GOLD STREET (BETWEEN PACIFIC AND JACKSON) (415) 433-6300

Whether you are in the mood to celebrate, flirt, or just enjoy an evening out on the town, Bix is an obvious destination. This is because the restaurant manages to be both bustling and intimate at the same time. This is not an easy task, but Bix carries it off with vigor and class. The walk through the hidden alleyway that leads to Bix's front portal is an adventure in itself — you feel as if you are on your way to a speakeasy. Bix's swanky 1920's décor and sophisticated, well-dressed crowd give the impression that Bix is a fancy private club. And what a club it is! You can stand at the bar sipping your drink while chatting up the beautiful people there. And if you can get a dinner reservation, you can enjoy a delicious meal off the supper club menu while being intoxicated by the live jazz playing in the background.

Bizou

598 FOURTH STREET (AT BRANNAN STREET) (415) 543-2222

Bizou is quite noticeable from its Fourth Street corner in SOMA because its moniker is painted on its facade in bold but tasteful lettering. The restrained flamboyance of its signage is characteristic of the understated flare of this inviting bistro. Bizou is full of charm and has a warm, almost contemporary take on rustic ambiance. The food complements this environment. It fuses countryside French and Italian farmhouse cuisine with Mediterranean. You get the impression that Bizou is frequented mostly by regulars. No doubt this is due in large part to one of the friendliest and most knowledgeable staffs to be found in all of San Francisco.

Café Jacqueline

1454 GRANT AVENUE (BETWEEN GREEN AND UNION) (415) 981-5565

The North Beach section of San Francisco, with its bohemian roots, is kind of a West Coast version of New York's Greenwich Village. It is home to a plethora of moderately priced Italian eateries and cafés that cater primarily to out-of-towners. However, among all this clutter is a quaint and romantic restaurant known simply as Café Jacqueline. This quiet and homey space is open only Wednesday through Sunday and, more importantly, only serves soufflés. The soufflé ingredients are apt to change depending on the mood of chef/owner, Jacqueline Margulis. Her wonderful soufflés might include Gruyere cheese and salmon or prosciutto and mushrooms. For dessert, try the white chocolate soufflé. One taste will guarantee a return visit. The soufflés are prepared for two people — a very good excuse to bring someone special to Café Jacqueline.

Café Mozart

708 BUSH STREET (415) 391-8480

Café Mozart bills itself as "San Francisco's most romantic European restaurant." Actually, that might be correct. According to any definition of "romantic," Café Mozart is right on the money. Guests dine in an intimate, fairy tale setting that includes lacy curtains, beautiful floral arrangements, and carefully selected antiques that appear to be heirlooms passed down from ancestors of wealth and good taste. Though the atmosphere seems an eclectic blend of European styles, the menu is traditionally French. Choose from a delectable assortment of dishes that includes Chicken Dijonnaise and crepes filled with shredded duck. Dine while classical music plays lightly in the background, adding to the romantic charm of this cozy Nob Hill restaurant. Eminently suitable for special-occasion dinners, Café Mozart is a worthy spot to pop the question to your true love.

Far East Café

631 GRANT AVENUE (415) 982-3245

San Francisco's Chinatown is, naturally, full of restaurants specializing in Asian cuisine. However, the crowds of tourists make a day in Chinatown about as romantic as a day at Disneyland. Thankfully, you can escape from the hustle and bustle of this part of San Francisco at the Far East Café. The Far East Café has been serving its traditional Chinese menu to patrons for almost eight decades. And while the place shows its years, visitors instantly fall in love with the restaurant's private booths, which accommodate couples and small parties alike. Each of the ancient wooden booths is shut off by a simple curtain and comes equipped with a buzzer that alerts waiters of the need for service. In spite of its appeal, the Far East is almost a secret; few guidebooks even mention its presence in San Francisco.

Fleur de Lys Restaurant

777 SUTTER STREET (BETWEEN JONES AND TAYLOR) (415) 673-7779

If your jet set invitations are few and far between and if you don't anticipate an invitation to a state dinner at the White House any time soon, you can still experience the elegant life of the rich and powerful at Fleur de Lys. San Francisco's celebrated Fleur de Lys is expensive, but worth what it costs. Touted as one of the finest restaurants in the U.S. (if not the world), Fleur de Lys is deserving of its high praise and worthy of its high prices. Chef Hubert Keller was the first guest chef at the White House under President Bill Clinton, and he and his lovely wife, Chantal, treat all Fleur de Lys guests as presidential. An opulent décor, with fine silk fabric that hangs above diners like a tent, creates a fairy tale ambiance that is enhanced by floral displays, four-star tasting menus, and service befitting a Royal.

FLEUR DE LYS
RESTAURANT
777 Sutter Street, San Francisco, CA 94109
Telephone (415) 673-7779
Facsimile (415) 673-4619

42 Degrees

235 SIXTEENTH STREET (AT THIRD AVENUE) (415) 777-5558

You might feel that 42 Degrees is located in a dubious neighbor-hood the first time you look for it. However, just as soon as you notice the Esprit outlet next door to the fashionable restaurant, you will know that you have arrived safely at 42 Degrees. And when you step inside, you will know that you have discovered something vibrant and exciting. What would normally serve as warehouse space has been intelligently transformed into one of the coolest eateries in San Francisco. The hip décor and dinner jazz at 42 Degrees attract an upwardly mobile group of black-clad movers and shakers. They dine, with great style, from a menu that boasts dishes such as Niman-Schell veal chop, pan-roasted chicken, and seared halibut, all garnished with exotic sauces and side dishes.

2°
42
TOURS
FRI 11:30·3
SAT 6:30·11
CH
ER

Globe Restaurant

290 PACIFIC AVENUE (BETWEEN FRONT AND BATTERY) (415) 391-4132

The Globe Restaurant looks like a small loft or artist's studio but is at home in its identity as one of San Francisco's hottest restaurants. Despite its popularity, the Globe is a great place for a date. With the vitality of a gallery opening, the atmosphere at the Globe also maintains the feel of cozy and inviting surroundings. Perhaps it is the tiny bar by the entrance that manages to deter a loud drinking scene. Maybe the rustic terra cotta floors and the skylights make patrons feel at home. From the dining room you can watch as Chef Joe Manzare prepares vegetarian risotto or a T-bone steak (for two) with potato gratin and grilled leeks. Even without candlelight and champagne the Globe wins romantic kudos for its subtle hipness and choice selection of dishes.

Indigo Restaurant and Bar

687 MCALLISTER STREET (AT GOUGH AND FRANKLIN) (415) 673-9353

Painters Ellsworth Kelley and Yves Kline garnered much attention when they painted blank canvases with varying shades of blue, a move that broke new ground in modern art. The Civic Center restaurant, Indigo, indirectly pays homage to the spirit of these artistic mavericks through the bold use of blue and its contemporary approach to preparing its new American cuisine. The indigo hues of the restaurant blend nicely with the hardwood floors. A cherrywood bar accentuated by subtle lighting creates a vibrant space and relaxed atmosphere. In the tradition of many San Francisco restaurants, the menu changes regularly with the seasons and available local produce. Visit Indigo to experience its creativity, charm, and romance.

Jardiniere

Jardiniere has assembled all the elements needed for a successful San Francisco restaurant: a former Rubicon chef, Traci des Jardins; a classy art-deco design conceived by San Fran's well-known restaurateur, Pat Juleto; and a clientele of movie stars and media moguls. Jardiniere's exposed brick exterior is somewhat hidden by beautiful trees tastefully strung with lights. Upon entering, the patron's eye is immediately drawn to a winding staircase whose silver railing leads to a second-floor dining space. Nicely arranged with banquettes and tables for two, the second-floor space overlooks the centerpiece of the restaurant, a magnificent circular bar that is creatively illuminated by a gold-domed ceiling crafted to resemble champagne bubbles. Silver champagne-flute ice buckets complete the motif. Jardiniere is bubbling with romantic appeal.

South Park Café

108 SOUTH PARK (BETWEEN BRYANT AND BRANNAN) (415) 495-7275

Though it has absolutely nothing to do with the incredibly popular cartoon television show with a similar name, the South Park Café is not without its own faithful following. And for good reason. This SOMA bistro is located around South Park, a little known gem of a park that looks as if it were lifted from Paris' Ile St. Louis and transplanted into the heart of San Francisco's Multimedia Gulch. Which is to say that you will feel more as if you are dining in a cozy Sixth Arrondissement bistro than in a Bay-area restaurant. Complete with a French décor, including a zinc bar and close-quarter tables, the South Park Café offers great food and a friendly staff. It is advisable to hit the South Park Café early in the week if you prefer intimacy, for it begins to bustle in mid-week with an excitement that is both stimulating and captivating.

Venticello Ristorante

1257 TAYLOR STREET (AT WASHINGTON) (415) 922-2545

For most of us, a weekend getaway to the Tuscan countryside is impractical. An enjoyable but less expensive alternative is a delightful meal at Venticello. Treat yourself to homemade pastas and fire-grilled prawns in the rustic setting of this Nob Hill trattoria. With its high ceilings, muted colors, and terrific light, Venticello captures the warmth and coziness of a northern Italian farmhouse. Others are well aware of Venticello's captivating Italian charm, so reservations are a must and a wait to be seated is to be expected. But if you must wait, Venticello has placed a little wooden bench outside the entrance to give you the chance to enjoy a glass of Chianti in the fresh San Francisco air.

Woodward's Garden

1700 MISSION STREET (AT DUBOCE) (415) 621-7122

If you have the good fortune to happen onto Woodward's Garden, you will experience one of the greatest culinary experiences in San Francisco. Nestled away under a freeway overpass, Woodward's Garden, at the corner of Mission and Duboce, looks as if it could have been an exterior set for Sergio Leone's *Once Upon a Time in America*. Its historic charm is due in part to the fact that it once housed J. B. Woodward's impressive and much-visited public gardens during the late 1800's. But times have changed. Presently chef/owners Margie Conard and Dana Tommasino turn out an eclectic menu of American and Mediterranean-inspired dishes that are sure to dazzle the finickiest of palates. From your table in the tiny yet intimate restaurant you can watch as the chefs prepare your meal.

Dame, a Restaurant

1815 MARKET STREET (BETWEEN VALEN AND GUERRERO) (415) 255-8818

Dame, as it is known by locals, follows its name with "a restaurant" probably because its presence on an almost nondescript section of Market Street might make potential customers mistake it for something else. Dame is a popular joint for Castro residents who appreciate a cozy, unpretentious eatery that serves regional American food with an Italian twist at reasonable prices. What is special about Dame is its warm interior. Sponge-painted walls, high ceilings, and sturdy wooden tables and chairs give the place a sort of romantic, rustic Tuscan "feel" in which patrons can relax during their meal. Dame's low-key atmosphere provides an ideal setting for brunch. A short menu ranging from pastas to French toast to smoothies will start your afternoon off with a smile.

The Elite Café

2049 FILLMORE STREET (AT CALIFORNIA STREET) (415) 346-8668

Just about every type of cuisine in the world is available in San Francisco — it's a sort of United Nations of restaurants. It's not surprising that this cosmopolitan city has embraced Donald Link's Cajun/Creole fare at The Elite Café. This bustling restaurant, with its customary hordes of people awaiting tables and the crowds usually gathered at the bar sipping bloody Marys and throwing back oysters on the half shell, might seem anything but romantic. But The Elite Café has a charm of its own. There is a kind of East Coast, Ivy League exclusivity evident in the restaurant's decor, elegant silverware and linens, uniformed wait staff, and old-boys-club-style bar. This elite atmosphere only enhances the experience of tasting such delights as the crawfish etouffé, the jambalaya, and the crabcakes with poached eggs and béarnaise sauce. If luck is on your side, you might be seated in one of several private booths that habitués of the restaurant vye for.

Greens Restaurant

FORT MASON BUILDING A (AT BUCHANAN AND BEACH) (415) 771-6222

Only in California — and maybe only in San Francisco — will you find a restaurant that specializes in "gourmet vegetarian" food. Such a place can be found in Greens Restaurant. Unlike most vegetarian restaurants, Greens is likely to appeal even to those who are indifferent to the benefits and pleasures of a meatless diet. Most of the seasonal ingredients are gathered from the near-by Green Gulch Farm, ensuring an extraordinary degree of freshness, before being artfully crafted into delec-table dishes that would be at home in any four-star restaurant. Ironically enough, Greens is housed in a converted military barracks in Fort Mason Center. But a tasteful Zen-like decor and a breathtaking view of the Golden Gate Bridge and San Francisco Bay create a peaceful atmosphere that is light-years from the exacting schedules and hustle of military life.

Lovejoy's Antiques and Tea Room

1195 CHURCH STREET (AT TWENTY-NINTH STREET) (415) 648-5895

Lovejoy was the main character of a popular British television series who owned an antiques store and found himself each week entangled in a web of mystery and intrigue. The show is kaput but its spirit lives on in San Francisco at Lovejoy's Antiques and Tea Room. Operated by a crew of British expatriates, Lovejoy's is about as Anglophilic as it gets this side of the Atlantic. However, there isn't a hint of English pretension or snobbery to prevent you from enjoying a wonderful "high tea" complete with scones and crumpets at Lovejoy's. Buckingham Palace it's not, but Lovejoy's will give you a taste of English culture as it truly is. The antiques that provide the setting for Lovejoy's can't be purchased, though the restaurant is one of the few places in America where you *can* buy a jar of Double Devon Creme.

Lovejoy's
Antiques
& Tea Room
Tricia Hollenberg
1195 Church Street
San Francisco, CA 94114
(415) 648-5895

Savor Restaurant

3913 TWENTY-FOURTH STREET (AT SANCHEZ) (415) 282-0344

Weekends should be a reprieve from the busy workweek, but even the most relaxed of us are still faced with one difficult decision — where to go for brunch. This actually can be an important decision, because unlike the typical rushed business lunch, brunch is a leisurely ritual that allows you to enjoy a good meal among friends and loved ones. With the importance of selecting the right brunch restaurant in mind, consider Savor. This popular Noe Valley eatery uses every day as an excuse to brunch. Depending on your mood and the weather, sit out on the shaded patio or opt for the comfort of Savor's southwestern interior. You can select from a menu composed mostly of crepes, omelets, fritattas, and pancakes. Specialties include crab cakes atop homemade biscuits with Cajun Hollandaise sauce and crepe-wrapped smoked salmon and dill havarti cheese. Enjoy your brunch — even on a weekday!

Ti-Couz

3108 SIXTEENTH STREET (BETWEEN VAAL AND GUERRERO) (415) 252-7373

Very few restaurants can maintain a following as devoted as that of the Mission District's creperie Ti-Couz. Many feel it has garnered popularity because it offers affordable prices in a neighborhood not historically known for its affluence. Fans, however, undoubtedly choose to dine at Ti-Couz (which means "the old house" in Gaelic) for the best crepes outside Brittany. Each crepe is made to your specifications, and you have a long list of tasty ingredients from which to choose. For instance, if you crave a hearty meal, the "crepe complete" (egg, ham, and cheese) will do the job. For a lighter meal, you can choose the ratatouille. Either way, you won't be disappointed. If you have a sweet tooth you will have a tough time resisting a crepe filled with coffee ice cream and chocolate and will certainly succumb to "The Tod," filled with apples, ice cream, and caramel. Ti-Couz's friendly and informal setting make it the perfect restaurant for brunch. The restaurant's popularity will ensure that you will wait for a table just long enough to make you anticipate having more than one delicious crepe.

Universal Café

2814 NINETEENTH STREET (AT BRYANT) (415) 821-4608

This difficult-to-locate industrial-style Mission District bistro is certainly worth the navigational effort it takes to find it. The exceptional food, including pan-seared filet mignon accompanied with Gorgonzola mashed potatoes, light pastas, and mouth-watering desserts, provides one of many reasons to try Universal Café. On a beautiful day you can bask in the California sunshine at one of the few sidewalk tables placed outside the café, but its real charm lies in its sleek interior, a decorative blend of steel, cherrywood, and concrete. Its unique design has made it the sweetheart of architectural magazines and its industrial look and feel has influenced the design of many new restaurants. Almost lost in an area of offices, the Universal Café is like a small but chic Hollywood canteen. Given the stylish surroundings and crowd, it might just be.

Zazie

941 COLE STREET (BETWEEN CARL AND PARNASSUS) (415) 564-5332

The 1960 Louis Malle film *Zazie dans le Metro* is the only association one might make with the Upper-Haight eatery Zazie. The film depicts the adventures of a provincial ten-year-old girl named Zazie who comes to Paris. In its own charming way, Zazie (the bistro) captures the same lighthearted French spirit of the film. Inside the bistro hangs a small movie poster of the film along with other mementos of Gaelic culture. Weekend brunch is Zazie's biggest draw, especially when the garden patio is open, so expect a wait. In the same way the heroine of *Zazie dans le Metro* is fascinated with sophisticated Paris, so you will be with Zazie's alluring French ambiance and food.

Catherine Opoix
941 Cole Street • San Francisco CA
415•564•5332
94117

Alta Vista Park

TAYLOR STREET (BETWEEN GREEN AND VALLEJO)

There are so many things to do and see in San Francisco that some of the simpler pleasures are overlooked. A relaxing (and free) alternative to the city's other attractions is Alta Vista Park. Ensconced high atop the hillside where Taylor Street meets Green Street, the park is a little-known gem. You can sit on a bench in Alta Vista Park and stare out onto the vast San Francisco cityscape for hours. The neighboring mansions may deter visitors from familiarizing themselves with the park, but the winding paths and park benches are available for anyone's enjoyment. The park offers what are arguably the best views anywhere in the city. Day or night, Alta Vista Park takes romance to new heights.

The Big 4

1075 CALIFORNIA STREET (415) 771-1140

In a world of Starbuck's coffeehouses, Gap clothing, and McDonald's burgers, it is becoming more and more difficult to discover elegant and traditional establishments that hark back to the time when "society" meant "high society." There is Harry's New York Bar in Venice, the Café Florent in Paris, and, perhaps, The 21 Club in New York. These are places where elegant people meet for cocktails to discuss the stock market or yachting or a new play while apron-clad waiters tend to their wants. One of the few establishments of this class left in the world is San Francisco's Big Four restaurant and bar, in the famed Huntington Hotel. Located in the chic neighborhood of Nob Hill, The Big Four is Ivy League to the *nth* degree. There's lots of worn leather and dark wood and the ambiance is that of a refined private club. This is the place to bring a date if you are trying to demonstrate your sophistication — but wear your tailor-made suit and try to remember to act as if you were born to such refinement.

Caffe Centro

102 SOUTH PARK (BETWEEN BRYANT AND BRANNAN) (415) 882-1500

It may be quite a trek to the Caffe Centro just for a cup of coffee unless you live or work around SOMA's South Park, but it's a trek worth embarking upon. Bordering what is, arguably, San Francisco's most beautiful public park, the Caffe Centro is a perfect stop for a quick bite to eat or even a lingering conversation with a friend. For a simple lunchtime date over Panini or pastry, this place is a superior alternative to the numerous chain coffee shops that seem to have run amok in San Francisco. So grab a table inside or out and hang with fellow hipsters who can also appreciate the European charm of the Caffe Centro.

Café Claude

7 CLAUDE LANE (OFF BUSH AND KEARNY) (415) 392-3505

Café Claude is a must-see for anyone who longs for Poulet Roti or a glass of Merlot around a beautiful zinc bar. Café Claude is nestled away in a tiny side street known simply as Claude Lane (San Francisco taxi drivers rarely know how to find it) and is reminiscent of those pedestrian-only walkways one commonly finds on the Left Bank in Paris. Café Claude could not have found a more fitting location for itself in San Francisco; indeed, it is probable that no other such side street exists in the city. The food and décor are typically French, but the real charm of the place is created by the jazzy atmosphere and the ebullient crowd, both of which often spill into the street outside this charming bistro.

Club Deluxe

1509-11 HAIGHT STREET (BETWEEN ASHBURY AND CLAYTON) (415) 552-6949

"Old Blue Eyes" is gone but his spirit lives on at Haight Street's Club Deluxe. At many places the whole 1940's nostalgia craze brought on by the popular indie film, *Swingers,* is a bit contrived, but at Deluxe there is no doubt that it's the real deal. The authenticity can be verified in only one visit to watch owner Jay Johnson belt out Frank Sinatra tunes on a Sunday night. The staff is decked out in retro garb that seems to have come directly from the wardrobe department of *Chinatown* or *L. A. Confidential.* The martini-sipping patrons often participate in this enjoyable enthusiasm for all things retro, but you need not dress like a member of The Rat Pack to relax on the black leather banquettes and breathe the smoke-filled air of a time long past.

Hayes and Vine Wine Bar

377 HAYES STREET (415) 626-5301

With the California wine country so close by, it is almost surprising how few places in San Francisco have made it their mission to turn San Franciscans into connoisseurs of the wines of the region. The Hayes and Vine Wine Bar is an exception. The proprietors of this establishment apparently live to find, enjoy, and offer to their patrons wines from Napa, Bordeaux, and other areas of the world noted for their vineyards. Hayes and Vine offers a huge selection of choice wines in many varieties, vintages, and prices. It is also a very comfortable setting in which to indulge in the pleasures of wine. With its light wood floors, velvety seating, and ambient lighting, Hayes and Vine is civilized without pretension. It is the perfect place to rendezvous before dinner or after a performance at the nearby Civic Center arts complex.

The Orbit Room

1900 MARKET STREET (AT LAGUNA) (415) 252-9525

The decorative influences of The Orbit Room hark back as far as the Art Deco movement and the 1950's style diner and as far forward as NASA and the Jetsons. Basically, this popular and hip Market Street café falls somewhere between the 20th-century past and the 21st-century future. This might explain the cool crowd that frequents The Orbit Room. It is not uncommon to witness young and fashionable types roaring up to the Orbit on their Triumphs dressed as rebellious young James Deans or Marlon Brandos, nor is it odd to see more contemporary patrons dressed in Prada or Comme des Garcons ride in on their Vespas. Whatever the influences and enthusiasms of those who frequent The Orbit Room, all will find the café a funky place to stop for a coffee or drink in what are definitely unique surroundings.

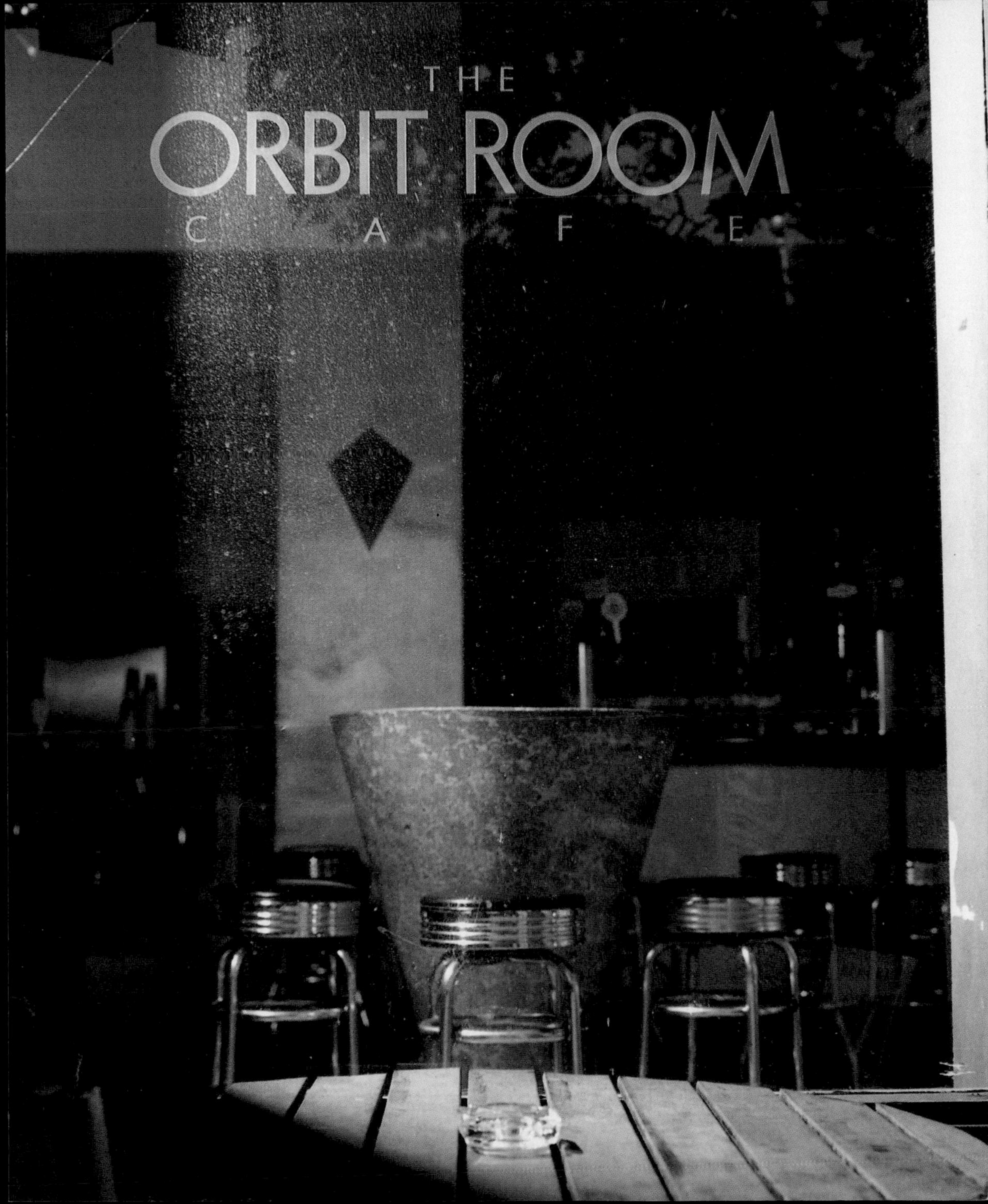
THE
ORBIT ROOM
C A F E

The Red Room

827 SUTTER STREET (AT JONES STREET) (415) 346-7666

For the past two decades theme restaurants, bars, and lounges have cropped up in such numbers that travelers can find the same chain establishments everywhere, even in small cities. San Francisco's counter-culture has reacted to this in the form of its now-famous bar and lounge, The Red Room. As the name suggests, the theme of The Red Room is the color red. Literally every inch of this exotic space, from the barstools to the banquettes and countertops, is red. This sleek theme manages to be neither gimmicky nor trendy, but instead attracts a consistently cool and youthful crowd in search of an alternative to spending an evening at a sports bar. And in the way that a beautiful woman is aware of her beauty, The Red Room is aware of its uniqueness. Try their Red Martini or a Real Daiquiri, which the cocktail menu firmly states is *not* frozen.

Roxie Movie House

3117 SIXTEENTH STREET (AT VALENCIA STREET) (415) 431-3611

"Art-house cinema" as it was once known, is all but dead thanks, in part, to the fact that the genre has become as commercial as, say, a Jerry Bruckheimer film. Luckily, there are still films that even the studios fear to touch, or fail to notice, thus keeping the avant garde on some sort of life support. One of the first and, for that matter, last, art-house cinemas is San Francisco's Roxie Movie House. Situated in the heart of the Mission District, the Roxie continues to project obscure foreign classics and hard-to-find independent films and documentaries. The 275-seat theater is relatively small by multiplex standards but is a perfect point of rendezvous for film aficionados and those tired of the mundane movie-going experience.

page eighty-three

Slow Club

2501 MARIPOSA STREET (AT HAMPSHIRE STREET) (415) 241-9390

Don't let the name fool you! Legend has it that the Slow Club is named in reference to the bar of the same name in the David Lynch film, *Blue Velvet*. However, on a good night, "slow" is the wrong word to describe the atmosphere of this out-of-the-way restaurant and bar. Like its sister, 42 Degrees, which is owned by some of the same people, the Slow Club lies in a seemingly forbidding industrial area. Set among warehouses and directly across the street from a depot that houses San Francisco's mass transit buses, its discreet location in Potrero Hill is part of the appeal that draws trendseekers and trendsetters from all over the Bay area. Its candlelit interior reveals the industrial style of the neighborhood: concrete floors and burnished steel executed in a typically modern and minimalist fashion. The Cal/Med cuisine is enough to spice up an evening at the Slow Club, but even an after-dinner drink at the back bar can do the same.

The Sutro Baths and Sutro Heights Park

EL CAMINO DEL MAR AND POINT LOBOS AVENUE

One thing that separates San Francisco from many other major American cities is its close proximity to the great outdoors. This is a quality that few San Franciscans take for granted because it is this very feature that has lured so many to the beautiful city in the first place. In a matter of minutes you can escape city life by taking a short jaunt to The Sutro Baths in Sutro Heights Park. The Romanesque buildings that housed the saltwater bathing pools opened in 1896 but burned to the ground seventy years later. Today, only the remnants of the buildings' foundations remain. However, the beauty of The Sutro Baths is the property on which it was founded — the surrounding Sutro Heights Park. Trails along the edges of the cliffs that border the Pacific Ocean provide spectacular views of both land and sea. In nice weather, Sutro Heights Park is the perfect place to hike and, later, watch the sunset.

CREDITS

PHOTOGRAPHS: Jimmy Hahn

PRODUCTION/PHOTO ASSISTANT: Stefano Pisacane

POST-PRODUCTION ASSISTANT: Lisa Dorffi

HAIR AND MAKE-UP: Annaliese McDonald, Billy Winters, Julie Brown, Ana Pineda

STYLISTS: Heidi-Marie Megyeri, Monica McKnight

INSET PHOTOS: Color Systems, Inc.

TEXT: William B. King III

MANAGING EDITOR: John Cantarella

EDITING: L. Lee Wilson and Barbara G. Carman

DESIGN: Robertson Design, Inc., Brentwood, Tennessee

Cover Shot	Bradford Gulmi, Yuliya Mock
Hotel Triton	Cory, Stacey Reed
Phoenix Hotel	Oz, Summer
The Sherman House	Stewart Asken, Csilla Erdélyi
Absinthe Brasserie and Bar	Bruce Wildman, Liliane
Bistro Clovis	Lisa Dorffi
Bix	Kristi Spierling, David Lurey
Far East Café	An-Ye, Amanda
Fleur de Lys Restaurant	Chantal Keller, Hubert Keller
Venticello Ristorante	Angela Noelle, Stefano Pisacane
Zazie	Susan Scherrman, Yuliya Mock Brad Gulmi, William King, III
Café Claude	Stephane Baumal
Club Deluxe	Jay Johnson, Scelestia I. Ove
Hayes and Vine	Jan, Yasminah
Red Room	Beau, Jessica Reeves, Laura

SPECIAL THANKS:

A | X Armani Exchange: *Leslie Appelbaum*

Orlando and Giulio Bandoni for the use of their 1949 Plymouth Special Deluxe

City Models: *Pink, Ken Moore*

Look Talent: *Alisa Hause*

Hi-Fi San Francisco